Your First COCKATIEL

Pages 2 and 3: Photo by N. Richmond

Pages 34 and 35: Photo by Robert Pearcy

T.F.H. Publications, The Spinney, Parklands, Denmead, Portsmouth PO7 6AR England

General

Most zoologists classify Cockatiels in the order Psittaciformes, better known to the public as parrots. However, the further taxonomic position, either among the Cockatoos or among the Broad-tailed Parakeets, remains a highly controversial issue which is best left to the experts.

THE WILD COCKATIEL

Some knowledge about Cockatiels in their natural habitat of Australia should help us to find suitable conditions for Cockatiels kept in captivity under different geographical and climatic conditions. On the other hand, let us not forget that most Cockatiels today come from domestic breeding stocks of birds acclimated for decades to the given environmental conditions. Thus we do not have to provide a miniature image of Australian conditions for our pet to feel well and to breed. We do, however, have to keep the Cockatiel's native environment in mind.

Wild Cockatiels are largely nomadic; they live in small groups in the more subtropical parts of Australia and in the dry grass and bush ecology typical in the inner part of the continent. Their diet consists of half-ripe and ripe grasses and herb seeds, which they can find on the ground, and also of green foods that grow during the lush rainy season, when Cockatiels normally breed. However, Cockatiels will breed whenever conditions are favorable, sometimes several times in succession. Nests are built in tree holes, always close to water holes or small streams.

Temperatures in continental Australia vary from well above 104°F (40°C) to below freezing at night. Cockatiels therefore are by natural selection quite a hardy species. Nevertheless, under the climatic conditions of North America and Northern Europe, they cannot survive without our help.

STRUCTURE AND FUNCTION OF BIRDS

Structure (anatomy) and function (physiology) of birds and mammals are similar, but there are some important differences.

Avian skin is very thin; it is devoid of sweat glands and sebaceous glands and is covered by feathers, which are occasionally changed during the process of molting. During molting, old feathers are shed and subsequently replaced by new ones. In Cockatiels, molting is a very gradual process, extending over several months, and it is often not even noticed by the owner.

The respiratory system of birds consists basically of the trachea, bronchi and lungs, as it does in mammal species. Additionally, birds have thin air sacs—saclike protrusions from the lungs into the chest and abdominal cavity—which can play an important, vexing role during the course of respiratory diseases.

The avian digestive system consists basically of an oral cavity, esophagus and crop, proventriculus, gizzard, and relatively short intestines. Birds do not have teeth, but Cockatiels do hull large seeds before swallowing them. The grinding of the food is performed by the strong, muscular gizzard that all herbivorous birds possess. This grinding action is helped by sand and small stones, called grit, which the birds swallow either as a matter of course or intentionally if they can find them. Sometimes lead shot, sharp pieces of metal, plastic, glass, etc., are mistaken for grit, usually leading to chronic poisoning or internal injuries.

The reproductive system of female birds consists basically of the ovaries and oviduct. The yolk is produced by the ovaries, while egg white and shell are added in the oviduct. The testicles of male birds are inside the abdominal cavity and cannot be seen or palpated from outside, as is the case in mammal species. Male Cockatiels do not have a penis. Copulation is achieved by pressing or rubbing the male and female cloacas together.

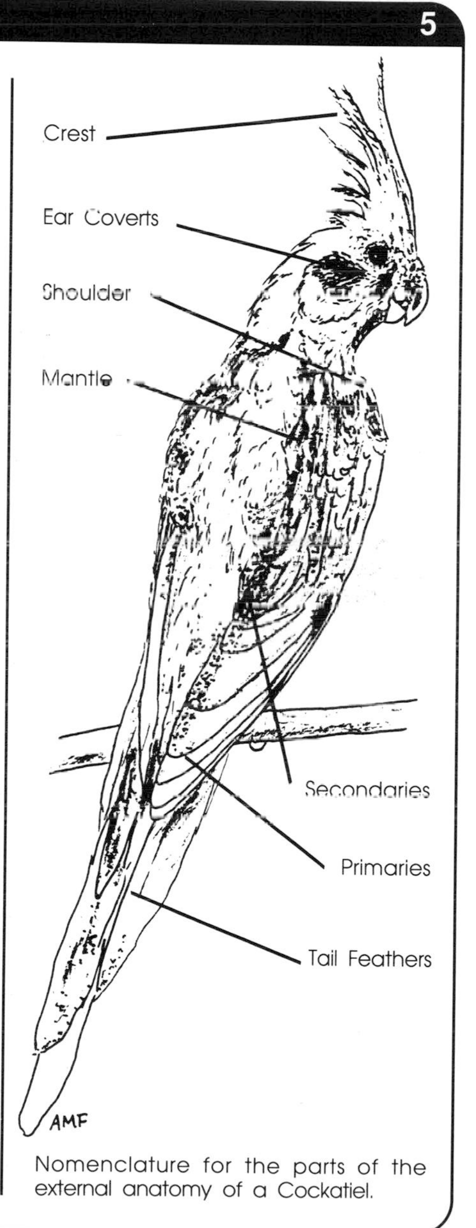

Nomenclature for the parts of the external anatomy of a Cockatiel.

Buying

To judge the health of an animal requires experience and a bit of good luck. Ask friends, other bird keepers, and your local veterinarian about reliable pet shops. You will still have to use your own judgment: What general impression do you get from the seller? Is the place clean, tidy, and draft-free? Of course, you should be comfortable with the seller, and his place of business should be as sanitary and well kept as possible. It is best to let the vendor do the handling of the animals; in this way you prevent accidents and can also gain a general idea of the seller's basic familiarity with birds.

HEALTHY BIRDS

Before getting close to the aviary or cage, stand back and observe the activity. Healthy birds are alert, hop from perch to perch, and show natural shyness when a stranger approaches. Lack of shyness is often a sign of illness, not of tameness.

Respiration should be quiet and even. An open beak, respiratory noises, and watery or creamy discharge from the eyes and nostrils are signs of a respiratory disease.

The plumage should be smooth and shiny, without feathering defects. The feathers around the vent should be dry and clean. Dirty vent feathers are usually a sign of intestinal or kidney problems. The droppings of a normal and healthy Cockatiel are green and firm with a white "cap," which is the material excreted by the kidneys.

The bird's condition is also checked by feeling its breast muscles. Birds with a sharply protruding breast bone are underweight and most likely ill.

Reject any bird with fluffed-up plumage, ocular or nasal discharge, defective feathers, crusty skin, dirty vent, overgrown beak, missing toes, or labored breathing.

SINGLE BIRD, PAIR, OR MIXED GROUP?

Often a pair or mixed group will be preferred because it typically means more enjoyment for the birds, and thus for the bird keeper—for no doubt it is entertaining to watch the interactive life and behavior of these cheerful birds. Wild Cockatiels live in small flocks, so mixing sexes is normally no problem, except during breeding. A slight disadvantage to pairs and small flocks is that the birds will spend more time with each other than with the owner and are likely to become less tame than would a singly kept bird.

Single birds may be particularly justified in situations, especially where a close relationship with a lonely, chronically ill or immobile person is sought. It must be

Generally Cockatiels are gregarious birds and thrive best with conspecifics. Owning a pair of these birds affords the watchful keeper countless hours of diversion. Photo by N. Richmond.

remembered that Cockatiels with no other living contact need a lot of attention from their human owner. Birds left alone for long periods of time tend to become frustrated and depressed, and they might start plucking their own feathers. Once a bird has started this plucking vice, it is almost impossible to rid the habit.

SEXING THE COCKATIEL

Considering the sex of a singly kept Cockatiel should really not be of great concern to the potential owner, as both sexes make nice pets. If you want a breeding pair, however, sexing becomes of vital importance, of course.

Sexing Cockatiels, particularly young ones, is difficult and best left to the experts. Yet, adult males of the "normal" wild-type are relatively easy to distinguish from adult females: the males have a yellow head and a crest with bright orange ear patches, while the hens have a more grayish head and ear patches that are less bright orange. Furthermore, adult females possess a yellow pigmentation on the primary wing feathers and on the undersurface of the tail feathers. However, these differences in wild-type Cockatiels are not visible until after the first molt, which is between three and nine months of age. Until then, young males resemble the adult females. This is unfortunate because the best time to acquire a Cockatiel is when it is still young. Mating behavior is a further indication of a bird's sex: male birds will try to mate ("tread") the female partner.

Additionally, there are a number of other sexing criteria, but they are not always reliable and require a lot of experience and time for observation. If the sex of the bird is of crucial importance to you, veterinarians can perform an operation known as a endoscopy, which will permit the observation of ovaries or testicles inside the abdominal cavity. Under normal circumstances the bird should be spared this operation because of the need for anesthesia and the risks thus involved.

AGE

A Cockatiel is best acquired when it is still young, adaptable, and capable of learning. But older birds can also make very nice pets.

Determining the age of a bird is a difficult task, even for experts. Unlike many mammal species, birds do not possess teeth or skin wrinkles that can indicate the age of the individual. Young chicks have somewhat duller colors and shorter tail feathers than adult individuals. The skin around the nostrils (cere) is pink during the first months and then turns progressively gray-black thereafter, except in Lutinos and Red-eyed Silver Cockatiels, where the cere remains pink.

In very old birds, the leg scales and plumage lose their shiny appearance, movements slow down, and keeping balance on the perch becomes increasingly difficult. Some joints, particularly foot joints, may be swollen due to gout.

COLOR MUTATIONS

A number of interesting mutations of the wild-type Cockatiel have appeared in recent decades. The first mutation was the Pied Cockatiel, sometimes also referred to as Harlequin, in which the color varies from predominantly gray to almost white.

The Lutino was first bred in Florida. The color is pale lemon; the gray color is completely lost, but the orange ear patches are retained. Lutinos are not albinos.

Pearls are a lutino mutation. They show a varying amount of gray feathers within the lemon-colored plumage. Cocks lose most of this pearled appearance after their first molt and will then resemble the normal wild-type Cockatiel.

Other mutations are the pale brownish Cinnamon, Red-eyed Silver, White-faced, and Blue Cockatiels, as well as others.

These mutants are attractive birds but offer no advantages other than color over the standard wild-type Cockatiel.

TRANSPORT, QUARANTINE, AND SOCIAL BEHAVIOR

The transport container or cage should be draft-free and strong enough to withstand the biting action of your new pet's beak.

If you already have other birds, keep the newcomer separate and under observation (quarantine) until you are convinced of its health. Sick birds must not be allowed to join the healthy ones. Nevertheless, even quarantined birds may be disease carriers without showing symptoms and must be observed diligently even after joining the other birds. Apart from the danger of infectious diseases, the new birds may also have problems adjusting to their new environment and may be harassed by other birds or prove to be rowdy themselves. Placing the newcomer in a small cage within the aviary for just a few days may help to prevent some of these adjustment problems.

MIXING WITH OTHER AVIAN SPECIES

Cockatiels are normally quite peaceful birds, but there may be arguments about partners and good nesting spots among Cockatiels. Cockatiels mix well with many other small avian species, such as Canaries, Budgerigars, finches, and other small parrots, but they should be kept separate from larger psittacine birds, which may attack them.

MIXING WITH OTHER PETS

Cockatiels may be kept with docile dogs, if the dogs are trained to leave them alone. If you have cats in the house, Cockatiels should be caged permanently. Mixing Cockatiels with guinea pigs should be no problem, but pet rabbits may be clumsy or hit back if disturbed by the bird.

Color mutations and variations in the Cockatiel have stirred much interest in recent years. This comely hen is a Primrose-Cinnamon-Lacewing. Photo by Michael Gilroy.

This colorful duo spends the afternoon sitting and chatting. Cockatiels appreciate free-flying sessions, a reliable partner, and good conversation. Photo by Isabelle Francais.

Housing

The Cockatiel needs a large roomy cage, at least 24x20x16 inches (60x50x40 cm) in size, in which they can spread their wings without touching the cage wire. Otherwise the bird may not get sufficient exercise and may become obese or otherwise unhealthy. Many, if not most, of the standard cages for Budgerigars are too small (even for Budgerigars!), but larger parrot cages will often prove suitable. The cage wire should be arranged horizontally on at least two sides for climbing, and the spacing of the wire should be narrow enough to prevent young birds from getting their heads stuck between the bars. Some parrot keepers and veterinarians dislike round cages because they are said to disorient the bird and to lead to circling disease. Proper furnishing might prevent this complication but would further reduce the space, which is already considerably smaller in round cages than in rectangular ones.

Metal is most commonly used for the upper wire unit of the cage, while plastic is used for the bottom unit. The bottom unit is either attached to the upper wire by means of catches or it consists of a sliding tray, which makes cleaning easier. Brass is a copper alloy and may develop a green deposit (verdigris) on its surface, which is toxic. Apart from this, some people feel that the golden appearance of brass detracts from the bird.

Timber and bamboo cages, commonly seen in Asian countries, must be avoided because organic material is very difficult to keep clean, offers hiding places for parasites and does not withstand the chewing action of a Cockatiel's beak. The reader also deserves a word of warning against freshly galvanized cage and aviary wire. Droplets of zinc, a toxic metal, may form and be broken off by the birds, who subsequently swallow them. Birds under stress are particularly prone to do this to relieve their excitation.

Screening or lining the sides of the cage prevents messy scattering of seeds and hulls. The liner material should not be made of glass and it should withstand the bird's beak.

SAND AND GRIT

Under natural conditions Cockatiels feed mostly on the ground, where they find the grass seeds that make up most of their diet. Therefore, Cockatiels should have access to the bottom of their cage. Metal grills, recommended for hygienic reasons, prevent this and should therefore not be used. The risk of catching an infectious disease from the droppings at the bottom of the cage is minimal, if the recommended cleaning procedure is followed. Also, most brands of bird sand contain pieces of grated mussel and eggshells for the bird's mineral metabolism and sand and small stones (grit) to help the gizzard with its grinding.

Gravel paper, i.e., paper with sand or seeds glued onto it, may help to keep the bird's toenails short but does not satisfy the Cockatiel's natural desire to pick and scratch on the floor. Neither does it soften the impact of the bird's landing on the floor, which might be considerable because the bird cannot make full use of its wings inside the cage. Therefore, the author recommends bird sand over gravel paper for the Cockatiel.

PERCHES

The usual perches of commercially available cages are made of doweled timber or molded plastic and have a standard-diameter. It is good practice to replace these standard-diameter perches with natural branches. For Cockatiels, the perch diameter should vary between 0.5 and 2.0 cm, forcing the bird constantly to adjust its toe muscles. The branch can be from a variety of deciduous trees, such as fruit, maple, elm, willow, beech, and larch trees, to name but a few. Never use branches from shrubs or trees with bitter or toxic branches or other parts. The branch should be free of droppings from wild birds and should be washed before being put inside the cage. Of course, branches treated with pesticides must never be given to the Cockatiel.

Apart from forcing the bird to exercise its toe muscles, natural branches also keep the bird amused and serve as an important supplement to the diet, because Cockatiels gnaw and eat the bark or rind, which contains nutrients. Once the natural branch is chewed clean, it should be replaced by a new one.

Perches should be arranged so as to permit maximum freedom of movement within the already restricted space of the cage. If two branches are at least 16 inches (40 cm) apart and there is no obstacle, such as a swing, between them, the bird has to use its wings in order to get from one perch to the other. Also, there should be at least 4 inches (10 cm) of empty space between the perch and the end of the cage, otherwise the tail feathers will rub against the wire during turning. Perches should not be fitted above feed or water containers because the bird may drop waste into its food and water, contaminating them.

NECESSARY ACCESSORIES

Necessary cage accessories include water bottles, food containers, bathing facilities, and cuttlefish bones. Toys can be useful if they offer your bird entertainment and encourage its exercise; but some toys are less useful or even superfluous, doing little more than taking space inside the cage.

The most common type of drinker is the plastic bottle with metal spout.

This type of drinker clips to the side of the cage and relies simply on gravity to bring water to the tip of the spout, which often employs a metal ball as a stopper. The spout must be made of a durable material like metal, as sharp pieces of broken plastic can be ingested and lead to internal injuries and possibly death. Clean the drinker regularly, as algae tends to grow inside it. Other types of water containers are open cups made of heavy plastic or earthenware materials. Drinking water should not be placed on the floor as it can easily become contaminated by fecal droppings.

The drinking water itself should be changed at least twice daily, otherwise certain bacteria (coli, staphylococcal, and others) get a chance to multiply rapidly, particularly under warm conditions. Water contaminated in this way may lead to severe and often lethal crop and gut infections, if the birds do not refuse to drink altogether.

Baths are either transparent bath houses or shallow tip-proof saucers placed on the floor. Some sand at the bottom of the bath prevents slipping. The water must be tepid and must be changed daily. Bath saucers should be removed after the daily bath to prevent further wetting of the cage. Refrain from using antiparasitic bath additives unless ectoparasites were diagnosed. Birds usually drink from the water in which they are going to bathe. Rather than a bath, tame birds will often enjoy a shower with lukewarm water several times a week. Do not shower your bird shortly before sleeping time and wet only the coverts, not the soft down feathers underneath. Otherwise your bird might catch a chill.

Feeders should be made of durable material (earthenware, heavy plastic) to prevent destruction and the ingestion of fragments by the bird. Usually the feeders are fitted on the inside of the cage, but some breeders like to offer the feed in a heavy, tip-proof earthenware saucer on the floor, because Cockatiels in their natural habitat feed mainly on the ground. The disadvantage is frequent soiling of the feed with droppings.

Single or small numbers of birds will be fed the usual seed mixture. For larger groups this may prove too wasteful because individual birds tend to develop a choosy taste, sticking to one or a few types of seeds, rejecting and spilling the others. Many keepers of larger numbers of birds will find it cheaper to keep the various seeds that make up a Cockatiel's diet separate, so there will be less waste. From time to time, blow the empty hulls from the top of the seed containers to make sure that there is sufficient feed left. Fresh or green feed, fruit, and vegetables should be offered in a separate container or clipped to the cage wire. Of course, fresh foods must be removed before they spoil.

Cuttlefish bone belongs in every cage. It is usually clipped to the cage wire. The bird uses it for beak

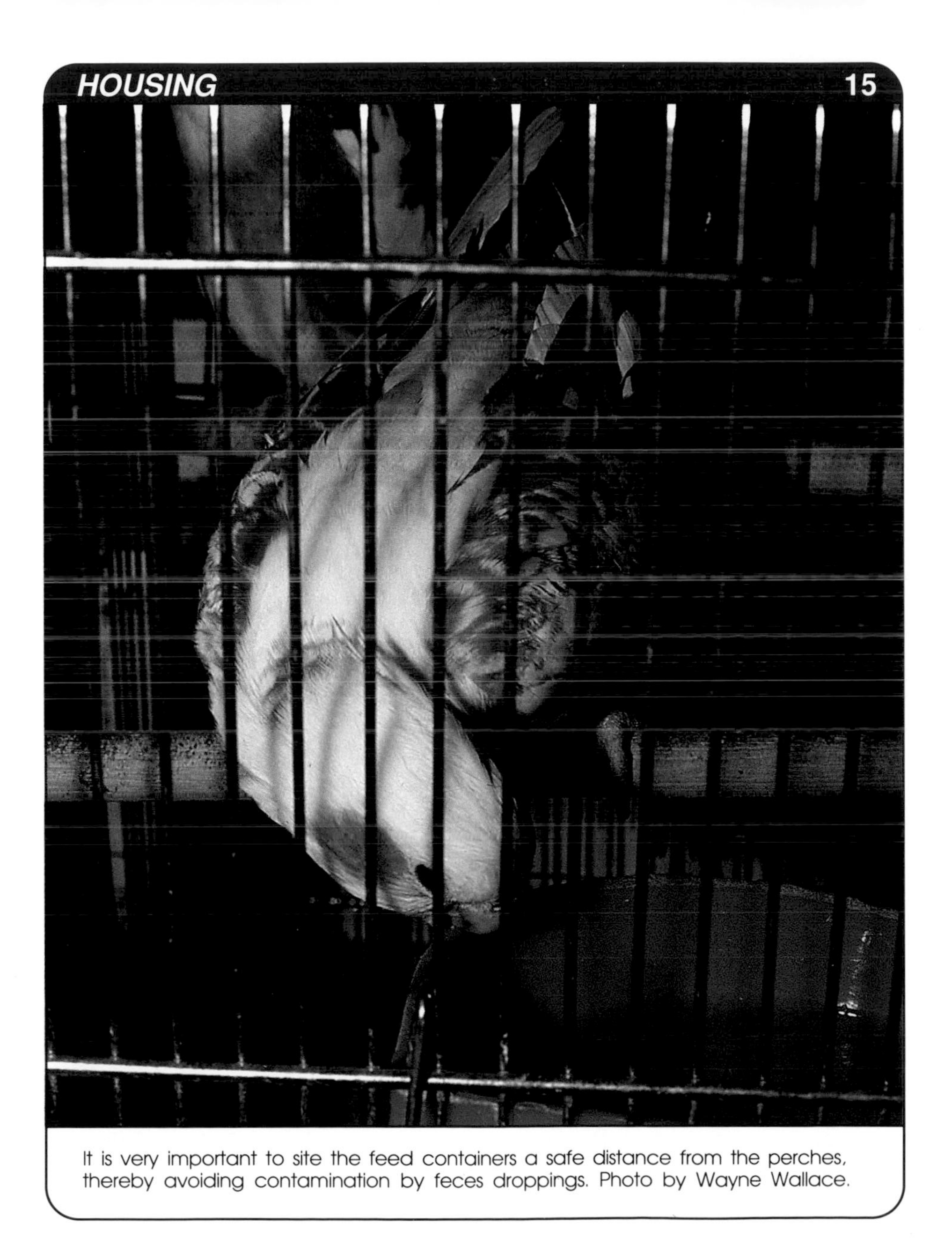

It is very important to site the feed containers a safe distance from the perches, thereby avoiding contamination by feces droppings. Photo by Wayne Wallace.

trimming and as a source of calcium and phosphorus.

A variety of toys are available for the amusement of birds (and bird keepers) at your pet shop, including entire playgrounds, swings, bells, mirrors, ladders, etc. As long as they do not restrict the bird's movements and are made of unbreakable material, they serve a useful purpose. But do not overload the interior of the cage.

Nest boxes will have to be provided for a breeding pair. They should be approximately 10x10 inches (25x25 cm) at the base and 12 inches (30 cm) high. They should have a shallow depression for the eggs at the bottom, an entrance hole of 2.4 to 4 inches (8 to 10 cm) in diameter, a perch outside the entrance hole, and an inspection flap on the top. A rough surface or wire mesh on the outside of the nest box facilitates climbing for the young Cockatiels.

Nest box hygiene is of critical importance to the survival of the nestlings and to their future development and health. Nest boxes should be easy to clean and must be cleaned and disinfected before each new clutch. Brooding temperature and humidity inside the nest box favor the growth of fungi, which can cause lethal respiratory infections. Large crevices and cracks may be responsible for drafts and chilling of the nestlings, and they offer ectoparasites good hiding places. Make sure that the inspection flap is properly closed at all times because chilling from above is a common cause of deaths among nestlings. The nesting material should be highly absorbent sawdust or fine wood shavings. Using dry peat or peat moss bears the risk of fungal growth after becoming wet because untreated peat contains fungi, and damp peat is a sure growth medium for fungi.

LOCATION

The location of the cage is very important to the bird's well-being: the bird must have contact with the family, and it must be located in a well-lighted, draft-free place that also offers a shady retreat. Birds appear to be less draft-tolerant than humans. Drafts can be checked by lighting a match or cigarette and observing the direction of the smoke: in draft-free areas, the smoke moves up vertically; in drafty places, it moves more horizontally. The number of places suitable for a cage is usually quite limited. The kitchen has too greatly fluctuating temperatures and holds too many dangers for safe flying exercise; halls are too drafty; bedrooms are usually too quiet. Also, the bird should not be moved from room to room. So, the most logical place for a cage is often the family room—where the television set is located in many households. Television light neither harms nor spoils your Cockatiel, but the bird should be several meters away from the set and out of the direct line of the screen.

LIGHTING AND TEMPERATURE

It was already mentioned that the cage should be located in a well-lighted spot that also offers shade. The normal light in a family home is sufficient. A dim light at night to prevent panicking is not mandatory but appears to be advantageous, particularly in places where sudden noises are known to occur in the middle of the night. Whether or not you should cover the cage with a cloth is a controversial issue, but covering it does protect the bird from chills. Under hot climatic conditions, covering the cage can be dangerous because the bird is likely to become too hot. Artificial ultraviolet light is normally not advisable: it might cause sunburn.

Excessive heat is unnecessary and often even harmful. Birds have no sweat glands and their only method of heat regulation is fluffing the plumage and panting. Anything between 63 to 75°F (17 to 24°C) inside the room should be comfortable. Extreme temperatures should be avoided.

EXERCISE

Most cages are too small to allow Cockatiels sufficient flying exercise. Therefore, your pet should be allowed regular flying time in a safe room. The Royal (British) Society for the Prevention of Cruelty to Animals (R.S.P.C.A.) even considers it absolutely wrong to keep Budgerigars permanently caged. What applies to Budgerigars is surely also valid for Cockatiels.

Before allowing a new bird to exercise in a room, the bird need be acclimated to its new environment and sufficiently tamed. Otherwise the bird might become frightened and associate exercise with a negative experience. The room should be thoroughly security-checked and other pets should be out of the room. Windows and doors of the room must be screened, dangerous spots (water-filled vessels, open fire, hot stoves, narrow gaps behind furniture, fans, etc.) must be removed or covered. Other dangerous spots are those behind doors, radiators, lamp shades, open drawers, spiny plants. Obviously, kitchen, bathroom, laundry room, and workshop are totally unsuitable exercise rooms for birds. Make sure that there is no access to toxic materials (e.g., tobacco products, drugs, alcohol, chemicals, ointments, etc.), or toxic plants (e.g., Christmas flower, lily of the valley, sanseviera, philodendron, cyclamen, oleander, azalea, daffodils, yew, juniper, privet, etc.). Do not rely on the bird's instinct to recognize all these toxic substances as life threatening.

Certain damage to furniture, curtains, lamp shades, wallpapers, cables, etc., may have to be considered. The droppings of healthy Cockatiels are dry and will be deposited only underneath selected perches, which can be protected accordingly. Cockatiels will not fly around restlessly but will spend most of their time on a few vantage points.

Returning the bird to its cage may

A sprig of spray millet spruces up a Cockatiel's day—supplements like this offer an excellent source of exercise, entertainment and sustenance. Photo by Wayne Wallace.

The lutino mutation Pearl is characterized by the lemon-colored plumage and the grayish cast to the feathers. Photo by Michael Gilroy.

be a problem at the beginning. If the bird has learned that feed is available only inside its cage, it will usually return to it without the need of catching it, if you have time and patience to wait. The cage door should always be open when the bird is out, with a perch in front of it. Catching the bird by hand should be avoided. Finger-tame birds will allow themselves to be carried to their cage.

OUTDOOR AVIARY

In cold and moderate climatic environments, outdoor aviaries should be built facing the sun. They should be dry, draft-free and have a shelter room. Proximity to industrial exhaust gas and smoke, busy roads, pigeon lofts, and poultry slaughter plants should be avoided. A concrete flooring stops vermin and a slope to the floor help maintain dry and hygienic conditions. Alternatively, the floor may consist of rough and fine gravel covered by dry sand. The sand must be clean and is best replaced every six months. Those aviary keepers who live close to sandy beaches and others who have access to plenty of clean sand should have no problem providing their Cockatiels with plenty of sand.

Construction materials for outdoor aviaries should be galvanized iron and narrow gauge wire. Preferably, the surrounding aviary wire should consist of two joggled layers, thus further preventing vermin and cats' paws from getting in and birds from getting their heads stuck. Be aware that freshly galvanized wire may lead to zinc poisoning if birds chew on it too intensely. If the construction material is timber, red mites can become a problem because they find good hiding and breeding sites in the cracks and crevices of the timber. This risk can be greatly reduced by applying a nontoxic paint at regular intervals.

The aviary should be furnished with plenty of natural perches, with at least two perches set at each chosen height to help prevent squabbling for the most favored perch positions. At least parts of the outdoor aviary should be covered by a roof. Without a roof, droppings from wild birds will land on the aviary floor, and these droppings might contain disease agents. If the aviary is only partially covered, make sure that feed and water containers are placed in the covered section. In cold climatic environments, care must be taken that the drinking water does not freeze in winter time. Water should be changed twice daily.

INDOOR AVIARY

Indoor aviaries are large cages that ideally allow sufficient flying exercise to make free-flying sessions unnecessary. Like cages, indoor aviaries should be well lighted, clean, draft-free, and heated, if necessary. Artificial light and a dimmer for the night should be provided.

Abilities

The Cockatiel is endowed with a number of skills. They are excellent and enduring fliers and climbing acrobats. They can mimic simple words and whistle tunes. Their speech is simple and less distinct than that of some larger parrots or mynahs. If you want to teach your bird to talk, start with two-syllable words with strong vowel sounds, such as "hello," "coco," "lady," etc. You may need a lot of patience, as you should not proceed to additional words or phrases until the first words are repeated correctly. When teaching new words make sure that the first words are not forgotten.

TAMING

Cockatiels are quite easy to tame while they are still young (a few months) and single (without mate or partner). Taming pairs and older birds is much more difficult. Most authors recommend wing clipping before starting the hand-taming process. Taming is more difficult without wing clipping but it is still possible.

HANDLING AND HOLDING

Birds must sometimes be taken into the hand and held tightly, i.e., for a close examination; trimming the wings, upper beak, and toenails; and for the administering of drugs.

Offer your finger to a perch-acclimated Cockatiel. Eventually it will step up!

Handling a tamed bird does not pose a problem. However, handling a nervous adult biter can be quite a stressful challenge. To handle an untame bird, put on a glove, close the windows, draw the curtains, dim the lights, and use a net, cloth, etc., for catching. Try to talk to the bird with a quiet, calming voice, and approach it neither in a hectic nor a threatening manner.

The best way of handling a Cockatiel is by closing the palm of your hand over the bird's back and wings; and holding the head tightly between your thumb, index, and middle finger.

Cleaning

Cage and cage furnishings require frequent cleaning to maintain hygienic conditions. This is particularly important for aviaries with large numbers of birds. The disease risk can be reduced or minimized by proper hygiene, but it cannot be completely eliminated. Infectious agents have several ways of reaching their hosts—via feed (salmonellosis, pseudotuberculosis, fungi), water (coli enteritis, salmonellosis), air (viruses, pseudotuberculosis, fungi), vermin (salmonellosis, pseudotuberculosis). It is obvious that hygiene cannot have any direct influence on metabolic diseases, but unhygienic conditions, and the stress that goes with them, might render birds more susceptible to such diseases.

Some of the prerequisites for hygienic conditions are cleanliness, tidiness, clean air, waterproof or at least water-repellent materials, and smooth surfaces. It would be much more difficult to keep a richly decorated bamboo cage (as commonly used in Asian countries) clean, than it would a modern cage with wire for the top and hard plastic for the bottom. Tidying up not only removes dust and dirt but also, and more importantly, allows for effective disinfection: disinfectants cannot work if the disease agents to be killed are covered, and thus protected, by dust, dirt, feces and other organic matter.

STEPS TOWARDS HYGIENIC CONDITIONS

1. Tidy up and remove grossly visible dirt, using a vacuum cleaner, shovel, scraper, wire brush, etc.
2. Soak cage contents in water containing detergent or another mild cleaning agent for up to 24 hours.
3. Clean cage with hard brush, scraper, wire brush, water; include the use of steam-cleaning equipment if possible, especially in outdoor aviaries. (Steam cleans well but does not sterilize well because it usually cools too fast.)
4. Dry all materials. Without drying, the water left from the previous steps would dilute the concentration of the disinfectants to be employed in the following step.
5. Disinfect cage and contents with one of the many disinfectants available in pet shops, drug stores, etc.

Most of the commercially available disinfectants are effective against viruses, bacteria, and fungi, but commonly less so against parasites. Active ingredients are usually aldehydes (e.g., formalin), alcohols, phenols, detergents, quaternary ammonium compounds, or a combination of these. Numerous brands are available, and to name just a few trademarks might prejudice against many others of similar effectiveness. If you are in doubt, ask your veterinarian.

If your birds are infected with ectoparasites, such as red mites, feather mites, etc., both the animals and the aviary should be treated at the same time. The usual insecticides that are used for this purpose must be handled with great care as they are also toxic to man. The treatment for knemidokoptic mites ("scaly face," "scaly leg"), which are rare in Cockatiels, is different because these parasites live permanently in, not on, the bird's skin.

Four Paws Mite & Lice Bird & Cage Spray is a safe and effective product for the fast killing of mites on birds, their cages and other areas.

Nutrition

The Cockatiel is mainly a seed eater, and its demands are relatively easy to satisfy. Pet shops offer a large variety of basic seeds and seed mixtures such as rearing feeds, tidbits, vitamin mixtures, molting aids, etc.

The basic diet of Cockatiels is similar to that of Budgerigars, consisting predominantly of sunflower seeds, varying amounts of millet, canary seed, niger, hulled and unhulled oats, wheat, peanuts, spray millet, hemp in small amounts, etc.

This basic seed diet is supplemented by different types of fruit (apple, pear, berries, citrus, banana, and other tropical fruits) and green food (dandelion blossoms and young dandelion leaves, chickweed, carrots and carrot leaves, lettuce, spinach, etc.). The soft garden lettuce should be used with discretion because it may cause indigestion. Firmer types of lettuce, such as endive, chicory, etc., should be preferred. The Cockatiel's diet is further supplemented by the rind of branches recommended as natural perches. The rind is chewed by the bird, keeping the bird occupied and supplying vitamins and minerals.

Some of the green food may be replaced by sprouted seeds, particularly in winter time. Sprouted seeds are especially important for breeding birds. Sprouted seeds are highly digestible and rich in vitamins. They are prepared by soaking the seeds in water in a strainer or in a humid container for about 24 hours. They must be kept in a warm place, such as in the kitchen, close to the radiator, stove, etc. After 24 hours the seeds are rinsed two or three times with tepid water and are left standing for another day or two, until the sprouts are just visible. Thorough rinsing after the first 24 hours is important for hygienic reasons. The warm and moist temperatures also favor the growth of fungi that are always present even on top-quality seeds. The process of rinsing should wash most fungi away. Do not feed sprouted seeds with a moldy smell or with visible fungal growth: they are likely to cause enteritis and fungal intoxications.

Apart from the aforementioned types of supplemental feed, there are other types. During the laying, breeding, and rearing period, the birds' diet may be further supplemented by commercial rearing mixtures, wheat bread soaked in water, hard-boiled egg yolk, small amounts of dried shrimp, cottage cheese, and tidbits such as honey sticks, seed rings, etc. Some of these types of feed are perishable and should be removed from the cage after several hours, depending on environmental temperatures.

Vitamin preparations are normally

not required if a well-balanced diet is given, as described above. Vitamins can be overdosed, particularly vitamin A and D. However, vitamins may be appropriately given for brief periods after stress situations and diseases. Let your veterinarian work out the appropriate dosage.

The same rule applies to various types of stimulating droplets and concoctions that are often advertised as an essential part of your bird's diet. They may boost your bird's resistance on a short-term basis, but given regularly and for extended periods, they usually have no noticeable beneficial effect.

Further components of the diet are sand, small stones ("grit"), grated shells, and cuttlebone. Since birds do not possess teeth, the seeds, after hulling by the beak, must be ground in the muscular stomach, called a gizzard. Grit helps to speed up this process. Grated shells and bits of cuttlebone are important sources of minerals for bone and eggshell formation.

Strongly salted or otherwise heavily seasoned human food, cheese, butter, chocolate, biscuits, and "junk food" should not be offered to Cockatiels, as they can cause diarrhea and obesity.

FOOD QUALITY

The assessment of food quality is a difficult and sometimes dicey task even for the expert. A professional analysis would not be economical under normal circumstances. However, there are several tests that can be used to give a rough assessment of the seed quality.

Reject any feed that is clumped, moldy, or wet, and of course any that contains vermin or their droppings. Always check the date of manufacture or harvest and also the country of origin.

Smell the feed at close distance; spoiled feed has a stuffy, stale, rancid, or pungent odor.

Taste a few seeds and check for the sweet taste of fresh seeds after you have determined that the seed is not contaminated in any way.

Sprout Test a sample of the seed, employing the method of sprouting seed as described earlier; 80 to 90% of the fresh seeds should sprout.

Oil Test a sample of the seed; a fresh seed pressed on a sheet of paper will leave an oil spot, while a very old and dry seed will not.

Rancid feed can be the result of prolonged storage, overheating during storage, direct sunlight, contamination with feed mites, and many other factors. Rancid feed can deplete the bird of vitamin A and E and can cause enteritis.

FOOD STORAGE

All feed is perishable to a varying degree. Feed components can be metabolized by fermentation, bacteria, fungi, and parasites. Some of these metabolized components are quite toxic, leading to diarrhea, liver damage, deficiencies, and other problems. Well-known examples of products that produce these undesirable effects are rancid fat and moldy bread. Since feed spoilage is accelerated by light, high temperatures, high humidity, and other factors, the rate of spoilage can be reduced by following these storage conditions:

1. Keep the feed cool, about 50 to 54°F (10 to 12°C) but not refrigerated to reduce condensation.

2. Keep the feed dry, below 70% relative humidity, whenever possible. Under tropical conditions, keep the feed in a ventilated place. Do not keep it in a tightly closed container for long periods.

3. Keep the feed dark, certainly away from direct sunlight, which would heat up the feed, cause fats to turn rancid, and inactivate the vitamins.

4. Keep the feed vermin-proof; mice and rats are often carriers of disease agents (salmonellosis, pseudotuberculosis); feed mites cause fat to go rancid; weevils and moth larvae are less harmful but also undesirable contaminants.

5. Keep the feed for only a short period of time—a few months only; buy fresh feed and check the date of manufacture to ensure freshness.

The above-mentioned precautions apply to the storage of seeds. Supplemental feed, such as fruit, egg yolk, cottage cheese, soaked bread, etc., should be removed and discarded after a few hours, depending on the environmental temperatures. Sprouted seeds must be prepared fresh every day.

Four Paws Nature's Little Greenhouse offers fresh, home-grown greens for birds to enjoy. Fun for the whole family.

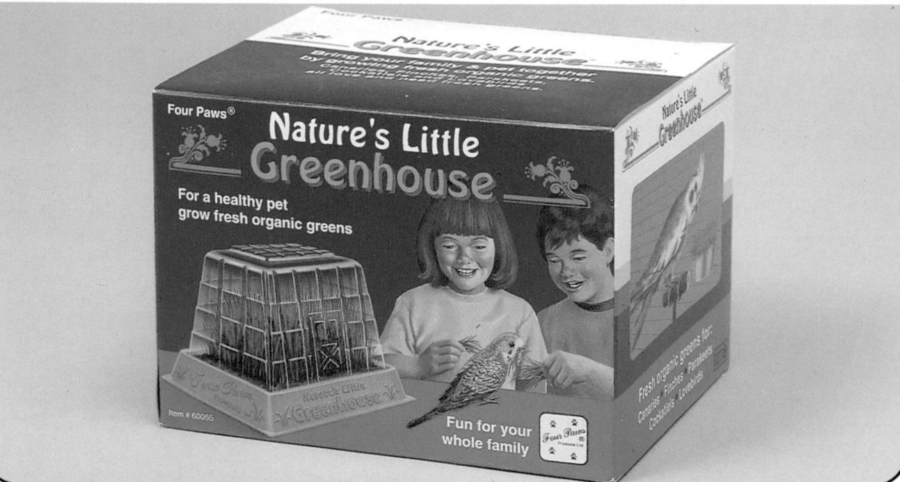

Above: Cockatiel seed diets are available from your local pet shop in assorted sizes. These seed mixtures provide a well balanced and nutritious meal for your cockatiel. Photo courtesy of Hagen Products. **Below:** Automatic seed and water dispensers are especially designed to hold the larger seeds found in cockatiel diets, and they let you always have a supply of fresh water available for your pet. Photo courtesy of Hagen Products.

WATER

Water is essential for life. It should be clear, clean, tepid, and free of chlorine, disinfectants, and any other additives. The chlorine gas of chlorinated water will escape if left standing in the open for a few hours. Disinfectants in very low concentrations are only justified if the water is not fit for human consumption. Disinfectants are irritants to the bird's intestines and may damage the natural gut flora. Boiling the water routinely before use is not recommended because boiled water tastes stale. If your water is of very poor quality, you can use nongaseous mineral water.

The drinking water must be changed at least twice daily, the containers rinsed out with clean fresh water on each occasion. Dirty drinking water supports the growth of certain bacteria, particularly. coli bacteria, and can cause severe crop and intestinal infections, which are responsible for many deaths among Cockatiels and other psittacine birds. Detergents should be used sparingly and must be rinsed off diligently because they can also irritate the bird's intestines and its bacterial flora.

It is often argued that drinking water is not very important for Cockatiels because in their natural habitat they can survive without water for a few days. This statement is misleading and dangerous. If the drinking water is not changed frequently, particularly during hot spells, it will evaporate, leaving a thick and often stinking broth behind, which may cause severe enteritis in your birds. Would you the bird keeper consider drinking a stinking broth instead of clear water?

FEEDING TECHNIQUE

Food and water must be protected from fecal contamination. Most commercial feed containers are protected against such contamination by a hood. Feed containers should be clipped to the cage wire and should not be placed on the floor, although some breeders feel that feeding on the ground is the most natural and therefore the most desirable method. Perches must not be fitted directly above feed or water containers. In aviaries with several or many birds, the seeds that make up the basic diet will often be offered separately to reduce waste. Cockatiels, like many other psittacine birds, develop very individual preferences for certain seeds and will spill the other seeds out of the feed cups.

Food containers must be checked daily. Empty hulls on the top may give the false impression that the container is still full. Empty hulls can be gently blown away. The basic feed, as well as supplemental feed—other than natural branches—should be changed daily.

Problems

There may well come a time when your bird is in need of professional help, when there is very little a layman can do. In these cases do not hesitate but go straight to the veterinarian. Transport your ailing bird in a small, softly padded, well-insulated box with sufficient ventilation; or in a small transport cage designed specially for the purpose and covered with an insulating cloth.

Post-veterinary treatment may include increased cage or aviary temperature, the application of infrared light, etc., depending on the disease or condition that was diagnosed. If you house several birds, it is a good idea to provide a "hospital" cage, also known as a quarantine cage, to help prevent the spread of disease and also to give the ailing bird a rest. If the bird is very ill, you should add an extra layer of sand at the bottom for the sick bird to sit on, and fit one perch close to the ground.

DISEASES

There are many diseases that can affect our Cockatiels, but fortunately few of them are common. Of course, in a book of this size it is impossible to list all the avian diseases, and equally impossible to offer in-depth coverage of any one of them. However, because awareness of disease is a vital concern of every bird fancier, the author provides here a list of the more common and/or serious ones.

Colds are characterized by nasal discharge, sneezing, fluffed plumage, and loss of appetite. If left untreated, colds may advance to serious respiratory diseases. Supply heat, avoid drafty locations for the cage, and consult a veterinarian.

Conjunctivitis is an inflammation of the delicate membrane that lines the interior part of the eyelid and the exposed parts of the eye. Conjunctivitis may be due to colds, drafts, local infections and irritations, or respiratory diseases.

Crop disorders, often associated with diarrhea, are common causes of vomiting and wasting in psittacine birds. Coli and other bacteria may be involved, and veterinary assistance should be acquired as soon as possible.

Diarrhea is a term used for the passing of wet droppings. It can be a symptom of intestinal infections (enteritis), e.g., coli enteritis, salmonellosis, or pseudotuberculosis. Other possible causes include psittacosis, parasites, and spoiled feed. Diarrhea leads to quick dehydration and requires urgent treatment. The passing of excessive amounts of urates (polyuria) may be confused with diarrhea. Consult a veterinarian as soon as possible.

Dirty vent is a common sign of diarrhea and kidney problems. A veterinarian should be consulted.

Ectoparasites are parasites living outside the host, e.g., lice, mites, fleas, and ticks. They are rare in Cockatiels, but they may be seen in crowded outdoor aviaries. Quick and thorough treatment is certainly called for.

Egg-binding is a condition in which the egg is unpassable through the oviduct. It leads to shock and local inflammation. If the egg is visible, apply oil and wait for the egg to be passed within a few minutes. Otherwise see your veterinarian immediately. Antibiotic treatment after removal of the egg may be very important.

Endoparasites are parasites living inside the host, e.g., worms, flukes, etc. They are rare in Cockatiels kept indoors, but may occur in crowded outdoor aviaries; they require immediate veterinarian-prescribed treatment.

Feather-plucking is a common vice in larger parrots, but it is rare in Cockatiels. Possible causes are boredom and dietary deficiencies, to name a few. Give plenty of green food, fruit, and natural branches.

Fluffed feathers are a symptom of many infectious and noninfectious diseases, indicating that the bird tries to conserve heat. See a veterinarian for proper diagnosis.

Molting is a normal change of feathers, not a disease. Young Cockatiels first molt at the age of about six months, and thereafter at intervals of once or twice a year. In Cockatiels, molting is a gradual process, extending over several months and often not even noticed by the owner. Extreme prolongation of the molting process ("stuck-in-the-molt") is pathological. It may point to chronic disease or nutritional deficiency. "French molt" is a feathering abnormality affecting mainly Budgerigars, rarely Cockatiels. It is caused by a virus and requires veterinary care.

Obesity is the excessive accumulation of fat and is related to overeating (due to boredom, too many tidbits, etc.) or to a lack of exercise, as when the cage is too small, perches are too close together, or there are too many cage furnishings restricting the flying space. Encourage, but do not force, obese birds to fly, and of course monitor and change their diet as necessary.

Old Age. The estimated life span of a Cockatiel in captivity is 12 to 14 years. Under natural conditions, a Cockatiel is unlikely to reach this age. An old bird may suffer from chronic heart failure and gout and may often have difficulties perching. For the bird's comfort, lower the perches, move them closer together, and add extra sand on the floor. If the bird suffers visibly, see the veterinarian.

Overgrown beaks are a common consequence of "scaly face mites" (knemidokoptic mites) in Budgerigars, and of a viral disease in

A well-trained Cockatiel can be given access to one or two rooms, provided that safety precautions are taken. Photo by Isabelle Francais.

Yellow-crested Cockatoos. Both diseases occur in Cockatiels, but they are rare. An overgrown beak interferes with proper hulling of the seeds and preening. The beak must be trimmed by an experienced person.

Overgrown nails are very common in caged birds, particularly if exercise is limited and perches are not sized correctly to offer natural claw wearing. Affected birds may have difficulties perching. Hold the foot under a strong light and locate the blood line in each nail. Trim nails with sharp clippers just below this point. It is best to have an experienced person assist you for the first few times.

Poisoning of Cockatiels may be due to numerous plant, consumptive, and chemical poisons. Poisonous plants include poinsettia, lily of the valley, sanseviera, philodendron, cyclamen, oleander, azalea, daffodil, twigs of yew, juniper, privet, etc. Consumptive poisons include alcohol, tobacco and other nicotine products, stimulant or tonic foods, chocolate in large amounts, etc. Some of the more common chemical poisons are lead, copper (verdigris), zinc, insecticides, rodenticides, most drugs, plastic fumes, etc.

Psittacosis is due to a virus-like infectious agent. Affected birds may not show recognizable symptoms or they may show general malaise with dyspnea, ocular or nasal discharge, or diarrhea. Psittacosis is transmissible to man, where it causes severe cold-like symptoms, often with pneumonia. Needless to say, prompt professional treatment is necessary.

Respiratory diseases in Cockatiels are usually the result of infections, e.g., colds, aspergillosis, psittacosis. Consult a veterinarian.

Salmonellosis or *paratyphoid enteritis* is a bacterial disease that causes general septicemia, hepatitis, and enteritis. The disease is transmissible from, and to, man. It is transmitted orally from infected feed or droppings from birds or vermin (rodents, flies, cockroaches, etc.). The disease can prove quite a problem in highly stocked aviaries, but is uncommon in single birds.

Vomiting may be a sign of crop infection and requires urgent veterinary attention. The bird may also show loose droppings (diarrhea) and may lose weight.

Wounds are usually the result of accidents or fights. Small wounds should be left alone, larger ones may need stitching or other forms of treatment. Separate fighting birds by removing the assailant.

SURGERY

Beak trimming is required in cases of overgrown upper beaks. The bird's beak must be kept tight and filed or cut short carefully. This procedure requires knowledge and experience and can only be performed by a professional because the beak may split or the bony structure may be injured.

Fractures are the results of accidents and are often associated with shock. At this stage it may often be more beneficial to keep the bird in a quiet place for a short time, rather than splinting the fracture immediately. The treatment of fractures requires the special knowledge and experience of a veterinarian.

Leg banding is not surgery but is used by breeders for identification purposes. Closed rings can only be fitted to nestlings between the ages of four to ten days. Narrow rings may later grow into the leg and cause necrosis of the part below the ring. Removal of ingrown rings is very difficult and requires professional equipment and knowledge.

Toenail trimming is required in the case of overgrown toenails. Care must be taken not to sever the blood vessel extending into the toenail.

Wing clipping is a painless method (if done correctly) of rendering birds flightless temporarily until feathers have regrown (after approximately six months). The most widely used method is to leave the outer two primary flight feathers and to cut the others. Other methods are clipping every other primary, stripping the vanes, clipping only one or both wings. It is important not to clip closer to the wing than the length of the coverts. Otherwise the quills may split and result in ingrown feathers.

Bibliography

THE JOY OF COCKATIELS
By Howard Richmond
ISBN 0-87666-554-7
PS-797
Audience: Geared towards the fancier who wishes to offer the optimum care to his pets and to receive the greatest enjoyment from them. This book prepares the keeper to tame and train his bird, maintain its health and vigor, and provide the ideal environment.
Hardcover, 5½ x 8", 96 pages, over 50 full-color illustrations.

THE ENCYCLOPEDIA OF COCKATIELS
By George A. Smith
ISBN 0-87666-958-5
PS-743
Audience: Surely one of the best volumes on the Cockatiel currently available, Smith's book offers expert advice on every aspect of Cockatiel keeping, maintenance, breeding, and genetics, as well as invaluable insights and information into the history of this fascinating pet's domestication, problems to expect in breeding, a guide to color forms and coverage of genetic mutations. The serious fancier does not do without this text.
Hardcover, 5½ x 8", 256 pages, over 150 illustrations in color and black/white.

THE COCKATIEL HANDBOOK
By Gerald R. Allen and Connie Allen
ISBN 0-87666-956-9
PS-741
Audience: The firsthand observations of the Cockatiel at home and in its native Australia by Dr. Allen and his wife Connie afford fellow fancier revelation and reward. It is clear that an understanding of the wild bird's behavior and the experiences of enthusiastic knowledgeable bird raisers are essential for the successful keeping of this parrot. Color photos in this text provide keys to understanding sexing birds and the development of young.
Hardcover, 5½ x 8", 256 pages, 175 illustrations in color and black/white.